KEY WEST NIGHTS
& other aftershocks

VAN K. BROCK
FLORIDA POETRY SERIES

ANHINGA PRESS

KEY WEST NIGHTS
& other aftershocks

POEMS

CAROLINA HOSPITAL

VAN K. BROCK
FLORIDA POETRY SERIES

ANHINGA PRESS
TALLAHASSEE, FLORIDA 2019

Cover Image: "Bahia Honda Rail Bridge," Carlos Medina
Author photograph: Carlos Medina
Design, production: Carol Lynne Knight
Type Styles: text is set in Georgia; titles set in ITC Quorum;
section ornament is a Charcuterie Ornament

Library of Congress Cataloging-in-Publication Data
"Key West Nights & Other Aftershocks,"
by Carolina Hospital — First Edition
ISBN — 978-1-934695-61-6
Library of Congress Cataloging Card Number —2018951939

Anhinga Press Inc. is a nonprofit corporation dedicated wholly to the
publication and appreciation of fine poetry and other literary genres.

For personal orders, catalogs, and information, write to:

ANHINGA PRESS
P.O. Box 3665 • Tallahassee, Florida 32315
Website: www.anhingapress.org • Email: info@anhingapress.org

Published in the United States by Anhinga Press
Tallahassee, Florida • First Edition, 2019

ON THE COVER: *The Bahia Honda Rail Bridge is a derelict railroad
bridge in the lower Florida Keys connecting Bahia Honda Key with
Spanish Harbor Key. Originally part of the Overseas Railway, the state
of Florida purchased it from the Florida East Coast Railway (FEC)
after the 1935 Labor Day Hurricane and converted it for the automobile.*

For all the women in my life
from Yoli to June –

Contents

Acknowledgments

Thank you to all the editors of the publications in which these poems first appeared:

"*Madre de Aguas*" first appeared in *Ethel 2,* September 2018.

"Carrion-Eaters of the Sea" and "Woman" were first published in *Illuminations,* June, 2018.

"By the Miami River" was published in *The Acentos Review,* February, 2018.

"Prologue" first appeared in *Saw Palm: Florida Literature and Art,* University of South Florida, Issue 10, Spring, 2016.

"Sea Horse Mall" and "The Pearl Necklace" were published in *Linden Lane Magazine,* December, 2016.

"Mourning Doves" was first published in *Raising Lilly Ledbetter: Women Poets Occupy the Workspace,* edited by Carolyne Wright, M.L. Lyons, and Eugenia Toledo, Lost Horse Press, 2015.

"Tamiami Trail," "*La Vacuna,*" and "Letters" were first published in *Linden Lane Magazine,* Vol.34, No. 2, 2015.

"Your name inside mine" was first published in *Linden Lane Magazine,* Vol. 30, No. 3, 2011.

"Southern Cooking" was first published in *The Miami Herald,* April, 1996.

Mil gracias, Holly Iglesias, Gustavo Pérez Firmat, and Silvia Curbelo for reading the manuscript and sharing your impressions.

So many individuals have supported me in writing this book, such as my Miami Dade College family, but special thanks to Maureen Seaton, Holly Iglesias, and Mia Leonin, who propped me up when I needed it. To my daughters, Nicole and Sonora, your incredible artistic talents keep me on my toes, incite me to grow. Carlos, without you, none of the poems would see the light of day, none of it would matter. Thanks for your patience, your creative vision, and your unfailing support.

Thank you to Lynne Knight, with whom it was a pleasure to collaborate, Kristine Snodgrass and everyone at Anhinga Press, who work so hard to consistently publish beautiful books to support the literary arts in Florida and globally. It feels good to be a member of the team.

Finally, I am grateful to my Catalan great-grandfather, Jose Hospital, who ventured across the Atlantic with his young family to become an immigrant in Cuba. As a trumpeter for the country's military band, in 1912, he played at the inauguration of the Florida Keys Overseas Railroad. I imagine him, trumpet in hand, Panama hat shading his face, commemorating this now derelict structure, the bridge on the cover of this book.

KEY WEST NIGHTS

& other aftershocks

The Rape of Rhythm

The rosewood waist of the guitar
presses against the drum hide
under the Ceiba tree.

Woman

She never rises before noon,
mornings disguise themselves as beginnings.
Better to trust the night's pledges:
      solitude
        stillness
        sloth

In the flat screen
      she reshapes the story

a surgeon abandons an infant
a fresh family in San Juan

      adjusts the plotline

19 year old girl marries
a twice divorcee
      28 year old alcoholic
      exile

      fiddles with the details

children   the Bay of Pigs
reunion   regret
nothing changes

      alters the focus

husband addicted to Johnnies
daughter addicted to Charlies
wife addicted to compulsions
binges
folds of flesh
numbness

      turns down the voices

that wasn't it at all ...
after the Cuban steaks
the highballs
the surgeries and Victoria
after the 50 years
that wasn't it at all ...

rewinds the climax

until she submits, eyes sore,
drained
3:00 a.m.

half a day closer towards sleep.

Psalm for Sisters

No more

cutting   despair

starving   hollowness

popping   sedation

breeding   loneliness

vomiting   famine

defecating   deprivation

lambing   breach

No more   marks

No more   labels

No more   trades

We are whole

Mourning Doves

Each Tuesday, she opens the drapes,
like a tabernacle,
to the trunk of the Sabal Palm,
a crisscross pattern of spiky leaf bases
splitting the second floor window.

How could she have missed
this hidden nest of twigs and dry grass
as she wiped down the window sill? She asks me.

The doves' soft grays blend with the frond boots.
Anyone could've missed them.

We lean over the granite ledge,
side by side,
gazing at the doves, awed
like toddlers, instead of middle-aged mothers.

It doesn't matter that since she departed
Oaxaca, she has only dusted
strangers' knick-knacks, like mine,
with only a 3rd grade education,
while I inhabit exile
besieged by words. We

wait for the mourning dove nestled above its chick
to move. The tiny beak
peeks from beneath its gray roundness.
The parent shifts to make room
revealing the young speck beneath
its long tapered tail. The mate

lands, opens its mouth wide.
The squab, head inside,
feeds from the glandular
milk. Both their necks stir in transfer.

Milagros

The wound is the place where the Light enters you.
— Rumi

Weekday car horns and the nurses' rapid
Filipino trill rouse me to the mist
                         over a nearby asphalt rooftop.

I wrangle my recliner muscles
shift back to fluorescent vigilance.

Washcloths of tenderness
wipe down her creases and folds untangling
sheets and hair matted with fever sweat.

One slips on socks beneath the blankets
like our mother before school.

Sedation drips swallow the gashing pain
of what should have been an overnight stay.

She swells up
                         a stranded seal

              barely alive
                         a fragile coral reef

more sedation

perhaps she'll forget long enough to heal.

Rueful in green scrubs
he finds us gathered in the waiting room

declares she will not outlive the night.

By her bed, a syncopation of dribbles
        mute rosary beads ... fraught strokes

her children's love whispers ...
              their repetitive arm patter

break through the hush and the haze.

For an instant
she wrestles her eyes open.

It's enough.

Blue

The slate burqa strewn across the chair
draws her away from the speaker at the podium.
Disturbed by the thick meters of cloak,
she refuses to try it on,
to even imagine herself confined inside the folds,
face concealed beneath the grille.

This shroud is a movable cell.

～っ

The speaker gathers the cloth layers
in tight folds. She feels a temporary
relief, to see it slip
back into the envelope marked:
Return to Sender.

Coffee Table Picture Book

War rages against women.

Karen gunned down today before her students
                    the man professing his love

Miro sorting through the remains of scorched
library books after the overnight raid in Sherpalam

Nameless a thousand —
Indian brides with sparse dowries
burnt alive, beaten to death, shamed into suicide

At the Chechnyan roadside —
seven young women
shot, dumped by the curb

Latefa and her sister strolling to school,
black pants, white shirts, head scarfs,
Afghan men approaching in motorcycles
acid spray blindness

On the border between Texas and Mexico
wooden crosses rising from the arid ground,
the only backdrop, telephone poles to Juarez

Lilia Alejandra, 17, not nameless —
her toddler waiting beside abuela —
abducted after a factory shift,
body shrouded in red dirt

In Congo captivity
Honorata strapped to a tree,
untied a few hours a day, to satisfy —
sterile, like Willermine
raped by rival groups
later abandoned by husband
Eleven month old Chaunce found
alive, her vagina mangled

Cream over the gendercaust.

Mothers and Their Men

Mothers whose seeds
are yanked from their fledgling wombs,
who recite rosaries
to their unnamed,
who swallow opioids with vitamin C
until their insides curl up,
who confess each night
miserable sins to hovering shadows,
they have been punished
enough.
Mothers who face
empty pantries
forced entries
discarded pill bottles
gnarled vows
exiled afflictions
beset by dearth
day after day
until ancient memories
displace their milkless swelling,
they have been punished
enough.

CHAPTER 1

You call me

Mutilated
Disfigured
Lacerated
Destroyed

                              Take it back

Your scalpel vocabulary
does not amputate
me

            I am whole

CHAPTER II

You ply me
with chemical solutions to

Bones
Gut
Brain
Ovaries

                              Take it back

Your cocktail lines
do not blunt
me

            I'm still clear

CHAPTER III

You brand me

Refugeed
Raped
Discarded
Damaged

                                        Take it back

Your shrapnel classifications
do not IED
me

                    I'm still here

Flares

Just as I'm drowsing off
    or settling into a conversation or starting dinner,
        a flare ignites my gut, shoots up my chest,
           and consumes my reason.

The glare sweats out my pores and smoke screens my thinking. The simplest utterance hurled my way triggers an altercation. I sense their eyes taking measure of my sudden shift. For a few seconds, no sound, no touch can reach me, not even myself. Seventeen years of flares, S.O.S.ings, still catch me, off guard. If not alert, I surrender to the searing burn within.

On the lucky days, though dying to tear at my clothes and plunge,
        I can sit still and let the rising dampness
                drown me.

Angela's Fate

By the wrought iron fence on Olivia Street,
an unkempt bit of cemetery,
hand written block letters on
a small stained marker
deflect the noon Key sun:

El Isleño
Manuel Cabeza
Died 1921

In the only grave out of 60,000 mounted
with dirt, among monuments for the victims
of the Maine and the heroes of the Wars of
Independence, rest unnoticed the vestiges
of this "tough mean hombre," a native Conch
from Canary Islands, a decorated soldier of the
Great War.

⌐

When Angela La Cubana sways down Thomas
Street, Manuel tracks the café on her skin
to her bedroom eyes, smooth sapote seeds.

His caresses don't unsheathe the wrath,
but his defiance, his common law
wife above his own
Red Rooster bar.

Wails of angels assail the Cayo.

On that dark December night
the fragrance of jasmine mixes with sea breeze
and spilled beer to flood the crimson room.
Hoods, bat in hand, strike Manuel,
arms pinned back,
they strike again
and again
dragging him to Petronia Street.

Stripped
      Whipped
            Tarred and feathered
Welts of rage run down his
back to Thomas Street.

Wails of angels assail the Cayo.

Angela curses the attackers and their descendants
to violent injuries, drownings, and fires.

Their worst offense:
      Provoking a good man to murder.

*Note: As the story goes, Manuel Cabeza, having recognized
one of his attackers, shoots and kills him in front of the Cuban
Club on Upper Duval Street. He is arrested. Carloads of
hooded men drag him from the cell, beat and hang him from
a tree, riddle his body with bullets.*

*It is said that his assailants and their descendants all suffered
untimely deaths.*

On Her 60th Birthday She Drives

I

*I came to see the damage that was done
and the treasures that prevail.*
— Adrienne Rich

There's no place to hide in summer
except indoors or beneath cool waters.
How swiftly the year has passed.
Loneliness issues its predictable sounds–
barks and whines–
her only refuge
rescuing the abandoned.
Hope emerges from the wreck.

II

*We are the half-destroyed instruments
that once held to a course.*
— Adrienne Rich

Crammed into the cruiser
four dogs, a camera,
she, and he, they and
the packed away
residues of their

        wreck

head to California from

        Florida.

If she keeps moving
across landscapes
she can breathe

        blue oxygen

windmills
overlook the heaves

until they reach the sea.

Madre de aguas

The dream spews elaborate tiles,
paladares and sobs.

Nothing is
        as it's supposed to be
                wood and water

The woman reaches
for this lament that pours over her
grips earth and tape grass
beneath the river.

Are my arms dissolving into sand?
My eyes rolling black pebbles?
My breath the current?

The Girl from the Hill

We arrive at a veiled El Posito before the rooster swaggers,
streets of ash, wooden houses flanking ditches:
the chapel, park, clinic, await light.
The SUV — heaving with duffel bags,
dentists, nurses, and an English teacher,
to organize the makeshift pharmacy like a Walgreens —
halts before the largest home.
In the back room I lie down on the twin bed
next to the girl from the hill, Cecilia,
a daughter's age, asleep, but not for long.

She rises like sunlight
                                without a sound
mops the tiled rooms,
stirs mounds of plantains,
cassava and sausages on the open coal, fire stove
under a high tin ceiling,
a meal for a queen
in this forlorn building
            half modern, with its cistern for the bathroom,
            half relic from a century wasted away.

                        Why isn't the girl in school?
                        In the afternoon,
                        after her chores,
                        my host answers.

I pick at the boiled yucca and onions
minding the child-woman hanging sheets,
relatives and neighbors nearby chatting in the carport.

The three siblings came down from the mountains,
impoverished padres entrusted them to my host,
work for schooling is the arrangement.

> *Why aren't you in school*
> *with your brothers?* I ask her.

> This gazelle of a girl refuses words
> like injury.

When I bend over to tie my shoelaces, my host fetches
the girl. I reject her help. She hesitates,
a gratitude glance shadows me across the street.

At the improvised dispensary I label and stack
stuffed baggies on temporary shelves
> from floor to ceiling
> calcium pills
> antibiotic pills
> aspirin pills, baby pills
> blue pills, red pills

body rows fold into a herd
nautilus arms grab me at the door
creep in through the jalousies
tug at my sleeve.

Cecilia frees me, her little brother
in tow; they sneak into the dental trailer
to exit later unfurling smiles.

We share a room for a week, side by side strangers.

On the last day, I thank her, tease her —
she must be happy to reclaim her space.

>   *Oh no,* she responds.
>   *I liked not being alone.*

In these hills lush with wild café and heliconias,
waterfalls and wading pools,
children carry such burden
parents discard them
to be raised below.

A Gray Christmas

This trip north to visit her sister,
she will not pick the plump berries
growing wild against the shingled house next door.
Not this time.
She hides her longing like the grime under
the edge of the window sills.
Carefully, not to spill a drop,
she carries the water bucket into the living room.
Mom and big sister pretend to fold clothes
in the back bedroom.
She's only 12,
but she understands the acrid whispers
between a broken heart and love.
She lifts the stained rag to
clean the old tired house near the sea.
The soot is so thick,
she only manages to smear ash across the wooden ledge.
Quietly, she toils
until exposing white.
No one notices.
From the second story window
she looks past the sandy path,
to the razed blackberry bush.
She scrubs each shelf, each blind, each
wall board as if she could
wipe away her beloved sister's disappointment
with her own.

By the Miami River

The scraggy woman with her half tainted
red hair inspects the heirloom
hallways sorting the missing furniture
wary
wary
The house molders
flanked by high risers
blinding
blinding
a garden parody
hungover pavers
cracked planters.
Inside
walls are crumbling,
tarnished pipes and rusted conduits
setting apart each room
conspiring
conspiring
She veils the light
with blanket curtains
until nightfall, when voices have quieted, she
sweeps
sweeps
sweeps
dirt from wooden planks
between the copper pipes.

Sitting at the Deli Near Work

for Miriam

New York poster walls
pumpernickel bagels
no one would guess we grew up
on yucca and café con leche,
before diabetes and cancer.

You are looking youthful,
slim in a rose silk blouse,
gray hairs concealed by auburn,
a slight spring in step.
So I am surprised when you answer,
not well, to my inquiries.
Fissures take on many disguises.

Is it normal, you ask me,
to feel such loss, still?
After all, college was the destination
we set for them years earlier.

Slowly, you butter your bagel
with care, I sip on ice water.
We talk about neglected dreams,
unexpected arrivals.
We aren't professors now, wives,
mothers, only two women.

Ahmed Kathrada and Robben Island

Your logic frightens me, Mandela
Your patience grows inhuman ...
— Wole Soyinka

Your will frightens me, "Kathy."
(Do I dare call you that.)

I see you
old man hunched shouldered, a father's smile,
pillar of patience, "tower of strength,"
Kathrada, Ahmed Kathrada.
(Is it a crime to chisel your name today?)
A H M E D !

I see you
setting out to Robben Island without the rage
of the long imprisoned at ferry gangplank
ticket in hand like a tourist.
How did you toss the gun muzzle hatred
(*Milicianos* in olive skin she'd call them.)
vanish the metal of bars, picks and shovels
picks and shovels, blisters and blood.

Your grace frightens me, "Kathy."

I see you
Virgil guide through hell's corridors
300 crossings after your release
each an ablution wrenching shackles
out of light retracing the fires.
(Not once have I yielded home.)

I see you
pure emotion taking on human form

you transmute exile colony of sulfur and beasts
into cradle, former fascist into friend
Christo.
Island misery slowly erodes years
of waves crashing against its trampled shores.

Your forgiveness frightens me, "Kathy."

I see you
old man without sighting of a single child
20 years, your worst deprivation, not a glimpse
of creator, but you do not stumble on barren ground
only mend stars and galaxies
in fellow prisoners and even guards.
Your reconciliation humbles me.

I see you
Island dung heap purged.

You frighten me.

Pipe Player

Father grips the bowl
begins to fill it steadily
in pinches
tamped down with fingers
carefully so as not to spill dried leaves
once
       a pause
            then again,
                 and again.

He strikes the match
circles it over
tobacco a few times
in a downward motion
as he draws on his mouthpiece
           long draws
                satisfied intervals.

As if measuring time, he rests,
the instrument
           his sole companion.

He drifts with smoke
           toward the open window.

At ease, he sets the pipe down on
the counter points
to his drafting table.

The Night Father Died

I started to leave the house that afternoon with a hint of a kiss and a "see you Thursday." When he hesitated, regarding me with confusion, I turned back to remind him, "It's Thanksgiving." I realize now that by then he had started crossing over, seeking out familial voices that summoned him. His body was frail, worn-out from struggle. When he fell from the mattress that night, gasping, he looked out into the vacant silence, as if eavesdropping on his favorite violin quartet. I'll never understand why mother didn't call us right away. By the time I arrived, it was too late. I sprinted upstairs to find his body stiff like the floor on which it rested. I found nothing, a desiccated gourd, an unbearable impersonation of a man.

Pentimento

Ahead
father
five years dead
baggy polo shirt
over stooped shoulders
random loose hairs
on his collar
staring at the floor
as if arguing with it.
He looks up. I don't
recognize the face,
only a brushstroke of memory.

Carrion-Eaters of the Sea

after Heberto Padilla

> The man takes a swim.

Buzzards — wings motionless — follow
in flight, August gusts,
sweeping spirals.
> An ocean is an island —

The gliding committee hunts
injury or malady.

The man turns in his hands
> fissured lines

his legs
> raw gunnels

his elbows
> crushed rudders

even his eyes.

The raptors grunt and hiss
> demand lungs and tongue.

The plumed wake assembles
but no feeding frenzy this time.

> The man takes a swim.

Corrosive vomit and
urine slither down to their talons.

An ocean is an island —

Featherless heads circle overhead
they venture down,
pick at the rubber boots
left behind.

December at Mt. Sinai

Spores spread like tentacles
until they tap his heart,
tangled with mine decades ago,
since he unearthed the matching pair
of gold twine wedding bands.

The size of an egg, the fungi wrap the valve
dangling,
threatening to lose their grip,
        to flood the valley that is his life and mine.

Time cannot be spared, I'm told,
they must eradicate it, now.
Do it! lunges from my throat. No,
not before the new messiah's birth,

no surgery until three days of darkness pass
without even a messenger.

I plunge into this river of red.
It drags me to the corridor window,
the constant ringing of excuses,
the pleading for absolution,
absences and assurances that
I do not need
        pillars.

I pace
        alone
                    tiles tear at my shoulder bone.

                    carts dismember my analogies.

                    fluorescent lamps conceal his gaze.

The scent of disinfectant
the frailness in his voice
                    the clenching at my throat
I must not whimper
nor wail

                    he must not hear

One Word
                    which claws at my ankles
                    gnaws at my will.

One antidote to this pilgrimage
a raging hold on hope.

By his bedside, in time, the flesh heals
but the taste remains

bitter roots.

Scenes from the Condo Front

The man walks the courtyard gathering
dead fronds and palm seeds
under the gaze of the red-shouldered hawk perched
on the black olive tree. He
collects empty clay pots abandoned
like stray cats.

～)

She hurls the object
at him, the one he has been tasked
to discard, an eye sore,
he flinches.

～)

He marches away to summon his boss.
Along the sidewalk trenches,
piles of old palm fronds lining
the property like land mines,
the ranting renter tracks him,
loud shrieks echoing
artillery.

～)

You fucking this and fucking that ...
She empties a magazine of verbal
ammo up and down the garden path
beneath the sea grape tree, its leaves
falling shrapnel.
A final *Bas-tar-do* she snaps in broken

Spanish – as if the words scalded her tongue
and his flesh.

⌒

Tight chested, he completes his tasks.
He padlocks the wooden gate mumbling
"good progress" and heads back,
a sentry returning to post.

Twin Force

for Carlos

The serpent coils and glides with
the twists of his wrist
turquoise with crimson scales
the ink beneath the skin winding
time's order.
Spiraling above the deck,
it pilfers the ship's brass bell
its line now in his grip
above the vein's swell.
No more alone
it dwells with him in permanence,
a shield of mighty clarity,
beside the beam's wake.

New Developments

after Alfonsina Storni

Curves
Curves and spirals
Curves and spirals and arches

Razed
Overnight

Squares and Angles
Squares and Angles
Squares and Angles

Wide flat planes
Consume   color
               rounded trunks
               winding shells
               shores
               souls.

summer 2016 bells ringing

Epiphany bells toll for the children of Nice ...

Colored fire in the sky, Bastille Day,
a truck plows into the easy crowd
(like a tank over wildflowers)
dragging the mutilated while their breaths still linger.

Eighty four lives traded for one
A dimming celestial Glow

shadow
ash

The bells strike...

Orlando full of sonorous gayety,
a loner, draped in bullets, bleeds them
(like a leech on a heaving chest)
 until he gets his fill.

Forty nine lives traded for one
A dimming celestial Pulse

silence
ash

All bells are hollow, so how to picture their sound?
(like ashes, falling weightless, but heavy
with consequence?)

A thought —

This is how the celestial one must speak (or it's how we listen)

Until the Beam turns to ash

And the Sound turns to ash

and more ash
and more ash
and more ash.

Prologue

He demands a poem in Spanish,
my native tongue.
I used to be a native.

I pry the calendar
from the waste basket,
the one bearing each month
a black and white photograph
of *la isla*
1957.

(Thank God numbers don't need
translation.)

Images of a childhood,
hotels, churches, bridges,
el tunel, la universidad,

but how do I describe the sound of the *batazo* at the
Coliseum or the smell of *humedad* in the Old
Cathedral in Santiago?

Snapshots, like a dream,
only I can't make out the colors.

Sea Horse Mall

Saturday mornings, after our instant Nescafé con leche and Cuban toast smeared in butter, we headed to Dadeland, then an open air mall. A 20 ft. dragon statue rising from the middle of a fountain marked the center. My husband insists it was merely a horse up on its hind legs. Perhaps so, but it was no normal horse. Small scallop shell looking wings jutted from its back. His muscular mounting image terrified me, almost as much as not speaking a word of English when we first arrived in Miami. The first months at the parochial school, I clung to my older sister's pleated uniform skirt waiting for the classrooms to open. When Sister Francesca arrived to lead the rows of students arranged by grades into the building, I reluctantly joined my own line, marching with my younger classmates into silence. It was mother who coached me every afternoon until the tears transformed into complete sentences in English. This particular Saturday our destination was Burdines. I don't recall what *mami* was buying, only her stern glare and stinging voice chastising me for correcting her stumbling words as the clerk struggled to understand her thick accent. Like the raging Sea Horse, she reared up against her fate. For years, she had tried to improve her own English with cassette tape lessons and community classes, but the Spanish trills and gutturals stuck to her like cane molasses.

Miami Poetica

Listen
Listen
Oyeme

Not to the words
To the sound

Listen
Listen
Oyeme

Forget that fucking iambic
City letters unravel in English
Chords obey
Childhood beats

Listen
Listen
Oyeme

Don't be offended
Grab
Suck
Fondle
Squeeze
Stanza after stanza

Tired of that unstressed syllable
Pestering me every page I turn

Screaming, my lines
Slap me
Hollering, they plead the pen

Oyeme
Oyeme
Listen

To St. Anthony and Eleguá

The visits play out like a high mass
first tía, then him. I was long married with

kids when tío arrives from Havana, Eleguá hidden
in one pocket a child born across

Florida Straits spellbound by abundance.

After extending the visa three times
he flies back to the island. Now

he makes offerings to return but
mother is too old and his mind is slipping,

ricocheted and disjointed. Ration books
transfigure into palomilla hangovers

bare shelves into rollercoaster aisles
of Trix and Fruit Loops where a resentful

Eleguá vanishes. Some days tío wakes up
praying to St. Anthony searching for

his red and black years favoring "The New
Man." Soaked in Malecón, he dissolves

into Biscayne Bay glare and outboard roars
sobbing mea culpas on mami's shoulder.

Perhaps we can't lose what was never ours.

Your name inside mine

        after Saints Francis and Damien

At Confirmation, you chose Francis
        your middle name
        drawn to his nature...
           his rejection of fortune
             his heritage
...a footpath...a renunciation

Exile.

Passed on to me   at nine
an open sore
Sister Helen marched us to the back of the school
a tucked away library
a threshold

the smoothness of the spine
the crackle of the opened binding
the scent of secret in the yellowing sheets

humility glued onto my ribs dangling under shirts

Before you met Francis,
I lifted Damien from the pages of that borrowed book.

A chosen exile of numbness

dressing ulcers, blessing disfigurement

dabs his silks on strange sores a string of puss   *shine*

You are my favorite lover of nature   *disabled*

you gravitate towards Francis
as once I did towards Damien
now discarded

You in me   ashamed of good fortune

*Note: Italics are from Nicole Hospital-Medina's poem,
"Confirmation Name Retablo I."*

Key West Nights

after Juana Borrero (1877-1896)

2010

I scour
tombstones again at the cemetery.
Her grave eludes me
like my family scraps
of war widow colonial
boarding houses
casa de huespedes and *repartos.*
Martí's widow, a carnation
that bleeds in the night,
beguiles Columbus
like Juana
nascent prospect of splendor
and genius
now loitering below
foreign soil.

1896

Juana is buried under Key West
nights three months after arriving from Havana
to folk she calls *cursi*

fishermen, rollers, spongers,
harried rebels,
wives and daughters

lacking the graceful inclinations
of a child raised among poets, a child
with an inward glance.

1877

Inside walls of canvases and recitals
she is born in *Puentes Grandes* –

outside unleashed chatter
of executions
seizures of supply ships, mothers,
desecrating students,

ten years of sugar cane fires and famine,
a machete wasteland

deafening for an infant bard
later coining verses to Apollo and
the daughters of Ran,
a mirror draped by a decade of
ravaged melancholy.

1891

By 14, Juana paints and publishes
verses, the Modernist poet
Casal seals this *sad virgin's fate* –

with the sadness of those
who must die early

his lace metaphors
and velvet rhymes
hypnotize her
a fog of idolatry and

unattainable longing
before his sudden death.

Desire expands too early
with reproach. It tears
deeply to tremble at its sight.

Ardor restored,
it is fleeting and forbidden.

1896

War resumes
news of possible detainment
drives the Borreros from *Puentes Grandes,*
Juana's academy, prison
of patriarchy.

At the bow of the Olivetti
she gropes for sight
of her beloved,
consummation morphs into severance
never a touch,
only dankness from sea
spray on *azabache curls.*

Behind, adored ground ...
ahead, the unknown, strange land, shadow,
cheerless night of postscripts and nostalgia.

Behind, a colonial capital,
of stained glass windows, intricate
grills, mosaics and grand
arches, of afternoon strolls along wide

promenades leading to marble
fountains and verses of medieval
troubadours and sad serenades.

She disembarks from the steamboat
ahead, sandy streets
two-story wooden structures
balustrades and feet
bare

cathedrals to smoke
timber pews of rollers
and the sweet scent of musty leaf

Key West nights

renewed chatter of war

now in multiple tongues
insurgents and
American soldiers
but no word of prohibited promises
cut off from her idols
exhausted from longing and doubt
consumed by typhoid
she dictates her last letter
and pens her last rhymes
of impossible love and a kiss
dreamed in nights of sorrows and tears.

2010

I scour
tombstones again at the cemetery.

Dusty sidewalks and rocking chair porches
mosquito netting on
humid nights and rooster crows
repulsive yet ingrained in her sensibilities
still surround the silent rows
of unkempt graves,
weeds and the occasional plastic flower.
Drawn within these gates
I stumble over dates and the familiar
names of unknown relatives.
Perhaps next year I will
uncover Juana
while rummaging for anything
to quiet my own impossible stirrings.

Backfire

For the three day voyage across the Gulf
ten men have designed a yacht,
a 1940's Chevy engine on a rusty metal basin.
The scent of soil a mile away
the boat engine belches black.
Boxed in, the vessel spins on the current.
The cutter impedes its way.
Like bull sharks
Coast Guards besiege the Cubist craft.
A bump,
the side of the tub dips.
Three men swallow the sea.
The rest,
exhausted by history,
are boarded, handcuffed,
defiled.
Another crossing awaits them,
back to a worn out narrative.

Still Letters from Far Away

The thin envelope turns up at our suburban safe house -

a long cursive return address, a tiny floral stamp from the land of

Cuban Oz. Back then no one came

just for a visit.   You escaped.

    With the yellowed parchment saved from better days, I imag-
    ined a black and white photograph Tía, pencil in hand, scrawl-
    ing her inventory of lamentations and shortages. First the
    daily trials: hot ration line hours, buckets hauled upstairs
    to the 1920's apartment, school walls painted for trying to
    emigrate, pillows dragged to clinic visits; then, the questions
    about us (a few); finally, the pleas for medicines, stockings,
    bras, soaps, vitamins,

            chiclets.

Today *mami* does not turn over the envelope to tear it open;
she tosses it.

She mumbles something, regret in her breath. I rescue it, slit it and
unfold the words.

Every inch of the sheet is blotched with depressed pencil
marks, even the margins. Tía always rotates the paper
to add last minute   forget-me-nots.

Postscript
Tía's letters stop arriving, her mind vanishing with her words. We
are told, she rocks, a blank stare, summoning her sister's name
across the Straits. Soon, she dies, discarded in a Havana infirmary
for the   forgotten.

New Year's

We pile into the station wagon for the annual excursion.
I ignore the flat landscape of Everglades grassland, barely
notice the occasional pine hammock, and am deaf to the
silence.

Home.

Now that papi has died, I cross the Everglades down Tamiami
Trail to visit mother, usually at daybreak. She lives near
island shore, busy rearranging closets or assembling photo
albums from long ignored pictures. As soon as I pass the
Miccosukee casino, I shed the concrete plains of Miami for
an endless sea of grasses.

I love when sunlight, almost level with the ground, smears
color on the wet prairie, so wide my mind's lens cannot absorb
it in one shot. Along the side of the narrow two lane road,
I catch quick glimpses of alligators, anhingas, white herons, and
the infrequent deer. Sometimes, hundreds of ibises assemble on
low branches, like feathered blossoms. I want to slow down
let my mind stroke their whiteness.

But urgency beckons me forward, to mother, waiting for the next
family visitor from the city. She used to travel back and forth each
week with her husband of 50 years; now she sits anxiously still,
surrounded by the artifacts of a once noticed life: her custom-made
walnut furniture shipped from Spain, her hanging landscapes and
Madonnas with their oiled tenderness, her dustless prized books.
Now, I cross these Florida pampas to alleviate her unmooring.

Fashion Alchemy

after Eddie Rodriguez

Trailing mami in her shopping outings for fundraising dresses, my sisters catch a few scraps: new school shoes, if lucky, or a sale top. The hunt doesn't appeal to me in my drab Catholic school uniform, a faded polyester blue. Papi and I deliver electrical drawings instead. College, 1978, I resist all but navy thick sweat pants doing double duty as PJs, or ripped jeans when the weather turns. Years unravel. Graduation. Career. I stumble through clearance racks or hand-me-down compromises from mami's wardrobe, silk blouses and pencil skirts, slacks and oxford shirts. I draw the line on tight suits or paisley dresses. They have nothing to do with how I imagine myself, nothing to do with the landscapes that bind me between Havana and Miami, pierced with shards of San Juan. My nemesis, fashion, with singular purpose denies me. One designer achieves what shelves of history books, family letters and recovered black and white photographs cannot: cast my illusive self-identity. An alchemist, he synthesizes my two innate selves, the exile one, with its American suitcase, and the imaginary one, with its Cuban bags. Home now is salsa skirts, finca hues, and wind chime earrings. They seduce and energize me. Without these, I turn into a cheap copy of myself.

La Vacuna

She wears the scar on her upper arm like a tattooed medal of honor she earned at four years old. Before boarding the plane she grabs her mother's hand, parading the evidence of the inoculation. From what? A tight grip is her answer. Under the other arm, she clutches her porcelain doll, with long curls and ruffled dress, gradually sliding. Long after the doll vanishes, the dime sized uneven edged mark provides access. La vacuna offers tangible proof she belongs.

Gypsy Chickens

The rooster crows, but it is way past daybreak.
Orange hackle feathers flaring, the cock poses
atop the tombstone's cross,
a princely overseer of his kingdom on Solares Hill,
with its cracked headboards and upturned slabs
butting against the few posh mausoleums.
His red pea comb shows up his black tail,
curved upright, stallion-like, fitting for this
cock fighting, Cubalaya breed, uprooted to
Cayo Hueso in the 19th century.
I watch him through the lens, but he turns.
Today his fight is with survival
among the geography of the dead
Key elites, veterans of wars, soldiers of the Maine,
mariners, writers, cigar makers, hung isleños.
Outside the fenced arena, many more island
roosters, hens and chicks, feral fowl like him,
peck at insects in drought dirt.
Along souvenir sidewalks and beer alleys
they dodge tourist bikes and scooters,
to brood on City Hall grounds and parks.
Their owners long gone,
their cackles and muck dispersed
by visitors or transplanted residents,
they multiply unattached to property or flock.
They have fended off hurricanes, developers,
Hemingway has-beens and outlasted everything and everyone,
Conchs, Northerners, Cubans, Bohemians,
Presidents, even chicken catchers.

Two hatchlings trail a black hen toward the hedge,
while across the street a roaming cockerel
reddens the asphalt.
They too have sparred and won.

*Note: Once a year, the Wildlife Center relocates about 1,500
roosters and hens from Key West to North and Central Florida,
prized for their eggs and pest control qualities.*

Florida Still

For Tula and Juana

Driven by wind stress
the current shadows the peninsula,
like rafters and Ponce De Leon, who rode it
north for they knew this river of sea was
more powerful than the wind in their sails.

Along these dunes of Florida shore
the stream always carries the island flotsam
north ...

Another goodbye in the works,
another poet packs, again,
propelled even further north.

The sea sustains its force
while the Magic City –
fades ...

So be it:
She will find anchor north
in less warmer waters
among oaks and pines instead of palms,
but still surrounded by infinite grains of sand and salt.

The Pearl Necklace

I was born into a middle class family of educated Cubans forced to emigrate for political and religious reasons. We carried no wealth when we arrived, but the aspiration and expectation of an upper-class lifestyle shaped in the United States. My mother suffered the inequities of being considered lower rank, not because of an inferior intellect or even career, since my dad was a practicing engineer, but because of language and culture. She often spoke of her own father, who died in Havana before she married, as a man of great insight and capacity, a judge, who spoke to her of the world, whom she felt in her heart could have been, should have been a diplomat, a representative of her small, but exceptional, island. Now she had to beg the monsignor for her daughters to enter parochial school and for the local civic institutions to allow her to volunteer. It was not easy being Cuban in Miami in the 1960's.

By 1976, tired of the tug-o-war at home, I married. We didn't have much, a used car, a tiny one bedroom rental, and two large tuition loans, but we were happy: independent, optimistic, and in love. Our first Christmas morning together, we gathered our presents and drove to my parents' two story house to open gifts with the family.

My husband's face beamed with anticipation as I ripped open his gift wrapping. The velvet box revealed an iridescent, perfectly white pearl strand, which made my mother shriek with pleasure. The smooth large freshwater pearls cooled my skin as he fastened the string around my neck. He was glowing with pride at this gift, a symbol of his affection and his accomplishment.

I suppose to him I was behaving like my mother's spoiled child, unappreciative and entitled, when I asked him to take it back. We could hardly afford our bills, how could he have spent so much, I demanded. He tried to explain how much it meant to him to declare his love, but I didn't budge. So he plodded back to the store dejected.

The story of the returned gift has become a recurrent comic tale at family dinners. Forty years later, I embrace the gesture of that young man trying to impress his beloved. Forty years later, I would have been delighted to gift that strand of pearls to my newly wed daughter. But back then, pearls pleased my mother, not me. They mirrored the life she longed for, that I desperately rejected. A pearl strand meant an apron and cribs, not the plan of writer and professional I had designed for myself. Becoming a wife was already a dangerous deviation, if I accepted the necklace, what would he imagine next?

La perra, el gato, y la flor

*for Maureen Seaton and Holly Iglesias**

The one you love is a one-breasted woman
on the cusp of an extraordinary day wearing
a Victorian nightgown, crumbs, buttered, sprinkled
atop the coffee table.
The orange red heliconia blossom falls
over the jasmine shrubs as she reaches
for the meowing cat tangled
among the stalks, her favorite morning song biting her ear.
The cat is not tangled but hiding,
the dog is hunting the courtyard.
The window pane shatters when she paints blue
heliconias on it. Every daughter
es una furia, the granite portico of her modesty.
The jasmine feathers blind the cat.
In real life, she did not go through breast cancer
alone. Beside her: Leonard Nimoy and José Martí.
Fickle breast
angeles weep.
They will snuggle under the hedge
after the rain storm.

*Note: This poem resulted from a collaborative experiment with
poets Maureen Seaton and Holly Iglesias. Other versions exist.*

Afternoon Love Poem

after Galway Kinnell and the 1970's

So spent
the scrapes of the long-married
ebb away
you make me feel brand new

fast asleep
you let the tip of the shoulder
            barely a touch
lean on me

mosquito netting sails
a fan breeze

drifting

a wooden sea
a mattress hammock

unhooked

a spark turned into flame

I can almost make out
Seal from the speakers
in the adjoining room
some lovin' here today
takes me back

our first clasp
young hands
under a beach wave.

Habitante 1970

What did I know back then
when papi called my date
to the eighth grade dance
a low life
habitante —

I don't even remember where we met.
I don't even remember his name.

Disco ball
Color my world
Bell bottom pant suit
                    liquid shiny purple
Pony tail tugged straight
          cast in hairspray
Does anyone really know?

Kicked out of the dance
Brass knuckles
Livid bruises

I didn't care
sitting in the car
first kiss.

Pinked

The photographer zooms in on the bay water

bikers quietly stand nearby
                    a drizzle

we pull over to join them, taking note
of this rare sighting in eight years.

A shrimp colored flamingo wades in the estuary.

Fixed on the bird's sinuous neck and posture
as its beak gradually reaches down to the shallow lake,
we note a roseate spoonbill nearby, sifting
through the muddy bottom.

The two creatures, alone in the quiet basin,
seem unaware of each other, or us.

We monitor the flamingo
                    stomping farther away.

The spoonbill, as if asking for attention,
suddenly
                    flies at us.

With its broad magenta wings spread open
        it glides right above our heads

        transforms the gray sky —

                    a pink embrace.

Southern Cooking

Like a courtly gentleman,
the risotto teases me
with its creamy blend of
rice and sunflower seeds,
smoothly spiced with shallots and
sun dried tomatoes.
With almost a side glance,
the risotto hints at nutmeg and curry.
Elevated "Low Country" cooking,
the chef called it,
"Southern Exposure."
I am truly hungry but I think,
not too much,
not too quickly, lest
I not be considered refined.
Then, I turn to the cornbread and
biscuits on the table.
They remind me of the scrappy schoolgirl
who stepped into our truck each morning
smelling of homemade biscuits
smeared in bacon grease.
This is home, I think again
and the coy risotto slyly
reveals the possibilities.
I dive into pleasure.

Love Worn

after James Wright

We are finally growing old
yet your graying hair
cannot hide the delight
of a 10-year-old boy.

For hours that turned into years,
the wind thrust its weight
against a bruised sky.
But the branch did not break.

Let us not scatter
like the autumn leaves.
One embrace will do.
For there is no loneliness like ours.

Being Juana Borrero

On our third hunt through the Key West cemetery,
combing the mislabeled map's marked areas for
an hour, stumbling over abandoned sites and
upturned tombs, we trip over the poet's
small gravesite squeezed between
an unmarked shattered cement
slab and a large white burial
vault. On her cracked
tomb, a donated
headstone
with only
a name, a
bleached
conch,
a minute
faded
Cuban
flag
and
now
dual
shore
stones
to mark
the waypost.

Transfiguration

Raspy squawks draw my eyes
upward. All turns to color.

Macaw pairs, paper kites
floating in afternoon glow,
wings radiant
                    stretch the sky cobalt blue.

They turn in unison
toward palms
their plumed chests haloing the sun.

Draped by green,
their talons grip the frond spines.
They balance ...
set and alert
guards at Buckingham Palace.

                    Better, at the gates of heaven.

Fruta Bomba

after Li-Young Lee

1

He says he hates their taste,
like a smack of fetid cheese,
still he reaches high up
for the green papaya with its
hint of color hanging from the tilting branch

because I love them

because he loves me.

2

Today I rush to slash the fruit open.
Mold like an old man's hair
has started to grow on its yellowing
pot holed white and brown blotched flesh.

One slice

the pitted center

a ripe Miami sunset.

Gifts

I don't recall when
we stopped buying them
we resist form and ribbons
roses withering into broken shards
chocolate dissolving into crevices
a Bond watch, a golden bracelet
when what I really wanted to give you
what I want to give you now
is turquoise
cool wide turquoise
waves of turquoise wrapped in sunlight
tenderness coated in dulce de leche
moonlight raised on osprey wings
I want to hand you
hammock laughter that can weed out sirens
our daughters smiles unhinging history's wrecks
dewdrop wetness and a love that binds.

The Way It Is

Scent of sweat
muddled with
a spill of bottled
gardenia
noon flesh
a dive into
iced tea sheets
cooled
a nap
in free fall
we rise,
still
dripping
kisses.

About the Author

CAROLINA HOSPITAL is the author of *The Child of Exile: a Poetry Memoir* (Arte Público Press); the novel *A Little Love,* under the pen name C. C. Medina (Warner Books); and *No Excuses! A Brief Survival Guide to Freshman Composition* (Sonoran Desert Books). She edited *Los Atrevidos: Cuban American Writers* (Linden Lane Press) and *A Century of Cuban Writers in Florida* (Pineapple Press). She also co-translated the poetry collection by Tania Díaz *Castro, Everyone will Have to Listen* (Linden Lane Press), and participated with 13 South Florida authors in the *New York Times'* best-selling novel *Naked Came the Manatee* (G. P. Putnam's Sons). Her work has appeared in numerous national publications, such as the *Norton Anthology of Latino Literature; Raising Lilly Ledbetter: Women Occupy the Workplace; Bedford/St. Martin's Florida Literature,* and *Longman's Literature: An Introduction to Reading and Writing.* She teaches at Miami Dade College, where she has been awarded three Endowed Teaching Chairs.